Touching the Heart of God

Cindy Barrineau Curtis

This book is dedicated to the unfailing love of God.

I thank my parents for teaching me to do my best and to keep trying. I thank my children for teaching me to think creatively and enjoy life. I thank my husband for teaching me to have the courage to write.

ISBN 978-0-6151-7466-2

All rights reserved. No part of this book may be copied with out permission.

Cover photos © Cindy Barrineau Curtis 2007

Copyright © Cindy Barrineau Curtis 2007

"Trust in the Lord with all your heart and lean not on your own understanding. In all your ways acknowledge him, and he will make your paths straight."

Proverbs 3:5-6

Life is hard. Period.

How we handle the hardships, how we live our lives every day, how we act or react when no one is watching determines our success in living to the fullest measure that God laid out for us.

Take this guide and be still with the Lord. Let Him speak to you in ways you never experienced before. Listen. Find the topic that you need for the trials and joys in your life. Let the words of the free verse poem wash over you as you remember a time when you felt as I did. Take your Bible and read the entire chapter where the suggested verses are found. If you do not have a Bible yet, read the verses carefully until you are able to get one. Ask God to open your heart to what He wants you to hear and know. You can take these thoughts and put them in a prayer journal to help you discover what God wants for you. Finally, pray the suggested prayer and/or add one of your own.

If you would like further study, a small group session guide is available. The searching questions are provided in the Appendix of this book. These can be completed very successfully on your own, but being with others and sharing support will enhance your experience and provide you with a network of support like no other.

The daily difficulties of life will not go away. The challenges we all face are difficult at best and can be overwhelming at worst. I wrote this guide to help you know that without a doubt, you have a God who loves you more than any other person has the ability to love. I want you to allow that love to fill your inner being so that you can live your life nurtured, cared for and ready for eternity. I want you to learn how to touch the heart of God in a deeper life fulfilling way. Finally, I want you to tell others of this great unfailing love. What can be more incredible than that?

Table of Contents and Scripture References
(NIV Bible)

Topic	Scripture	Page Number
Acceptance	Psalm 40:8	1
Adoration	Psalm 19	2
Anger	James 1:19-21	3
Blessing	Matthew 5	4
Change	Ecclesiastes 3:1-8	5
Comfort	Matthew 11:28-30	6
Confession	Numbers 5:5-7	7
Conflict	2 Timothy 2:24-26	8
Confusion	James 1:5-7	9
Direction	Proverbs 3:5-6	10
Discernment	Philippians 1:9-11	11
Discipline	Hebrews 12: 5-12	12
Doubt	James 1:6	13
Encouragement	Romans 15:5	14
Faith	Matthew 17:18-21	15
Fear	Psalm 91	16
Forgiveness	2 Corinthians 5:17-21	17
Gratitude	Colossians 3:15-17	18
Grief	Isaiah 61:1-3	19
Guilt	Psalm 51:1-17	20
Happiness	Philippians 4:11-13	21
Harmony	Romans 12:9-16	22

Healing	1 Peter 2:23-25	23
Hope	Psalm 42:5-6	24
Humility	Micah 6:8	25
Intervention	Romans 8:26-27	26
Jealousy	Galatians 5:25-26	27
Joy	Psalm 126	28
Knowledge	Proverbs 10:14	29
Longing	Psalm 119:81-87	30
Loneliness	Luke 5:16	31
Love	1 Corinthians 13	32
Overwhelmed	Deuteronomy 31:6	33
Patience	Ecclesiastes 7:8	34
Perseverance	Hebrews 12:1-3	35
Praise	Exodus 15:1-2	36
Renewal	Isaiah 57:10	37
Resentment	2 Timothy 22-26	38
Rest	Matthew 11:28-30	39
Salvation	1 Thessalonians 5:9	40
Strength	Isaiah 40: 29-31	41
Temptation	Matthew 26:41	42
Thanksgiving	Psalm 100	43
Worry	Matthew 6:25	44
Worship	Psalm 95:1-7	45
Appendix	Searching questions	A-D

Acceptance

Where do I belong?
where do I fit?
am I just a part of a puzzle?

Undiscovered

a place for me must lie around the next bend
must be at the next junction

Mold me
Heal me
Abide in me
Love me

A child
who is wandering.

Read Psalm 40: 8
"I desire to do your will, O my God; your law is within my heart."

Prayer:
God, I do not know what You have in Your will for me. I see where I am headed for just this moment, just this day and that is enough. Your plan for me is perfect and I cannot question why. Please, Father, give me the grace to accept what You have for me and the patience to wait on You. Thank You for loving me enough to guide me in all my ways. Amen.

Adoration

The glory of the Lord surrounds me
in the still quiet morning,
in the crash of the thunderstorm,
in the delicate lilt of the bird's song
in the majestic color of the flowers
in the rain sparkled evening.

I hear Your voice

as a whisper from a loving Father
"I love you, my child."
and I answer
in humble adoration
"Thank you, God."

Read Psalm 19
"The heavens declare the glory of God; the skies proclaim the work of his hands." Psalm 19:1

Prayer:
Heavenly Father, when I look upon the glory of Your works, I am so awed by the wonder of all You have created. The vivid colors of the flowers in bloom, the mighty ocean waves, the quiet of a gently falling rain, the highest majestic peak, all surpass my ability to fathom their wonders. You are the Almighty God, the Father and Creator. I worship and adore You, Lord, with highest praise. I rest assured with the knowledge that You love me in the midst of all the beauty and wonder of Your creation. You formed me and You love me as I am Your precious child. Thank You, Father. Amen.

Anger

The hot noise fills the space
inside my head -
a raging bull
ready to charge

WHY?

explodes from my lips
in anguish and pain
an unanswered question

one word

so full of darkness
and empty promises
will I ever be able to let go?
...and heal.

Read James 1:19-21
"My dear brothers, take note of this: Everyone should be quick to listen, slow to speak and slow to become angry... "

Prayer:
Lord of all, You know my heart is consumed with anger. I do not understand the depth of my feelings. I feel so out of control. I pray for peace and for your power to overtake the feelings I have and restore me to calm. When I rage and shout "Why?" Lord, I know You hear me. I understand that the answers to all of my questions may not be for me to know right now. Help me in my anger to accept that, Lord, and to rely on You. Thank You for loving me even when I am so upset. Thank You for taking my anger and working in me to restore peace. Amen.

Blessing

The joy
that wells up inside me
originates
in the endless waters of your love.

Wash over me
with the waves of blessing
more valuable
than any possession

lasting and true
grace
peace
and love

poured out for all times.

Read Matthew 5:12
"Rejoice and be glad, because great is your reward in heaven…"

Prayer:
Dear Lord, You teach us that blessings pour out on us when we live as Your children. I praise Your name and thank You for all the blessings You have given me. From the ability to wake this day and praise You, to the joy Your love brings to my heart, I thank You. I continue to need your blessings, Lord. I trust that You know what is best for me better than I do. I wait on Your blessings with a grateful, overflowing heart. Amen.

Change

It is too hard,
too much to ask,
too overwhelming for me.

The tasks set before me
loom large and monstrous,
too enormous for me to conquer.
I don't have the energy to try.

Change me.
Change my attitude.
Change my resistance.
…so that I am able
to conquer change.

Read Ecclesiastes 3:1-8
"There is a time for everything and a season for every activity under heaven…"

Prayer:
Oh, Lord, change is so hard. I do not want to go through this trial. It is too difficult to make the changes I need to make. Please, Lord, help me. Guide me to break down the tasks before me into small parts so that You and I may handle them one at a time. I can become so overwhelmed and give up before I start. Help me to move on today with one small step, then another and another. Most of all, help me to accept change and to embrace it with Your love and strength to hold me up. Amen.

Comfort

*The pain is
a tangible force that I cannot tame.
The depth of feeling
is unmanageable and fills me with dread.*

*I wait for it to pass,
it walks on my heart
tramples my soul
torments me night and day.*

I long for respite, for a moment of normality.

*I wait
wounded and fearful
for the promised hope.*

Read Matthew 11: 28-30
"Come to me, all you who are weary and burdened, and I will give you rest…"

Prayer:
Holy Spirit, You are the Great Comforter. You take my hurt and surround me with Your love. Take me now; wrap Your arms of love around me. I need the pain to ease. I need Your love to heal me and mend the brokenness of my spirit. You are the balm for my wounds and the comfort in my despair. I feel so helpless, but Your presence offers me hope. For the next few minutes, let Your peace flow over me in a mighty way as You relieve my worries. Take my burden and lift my load as only You can. Amen.

Confession

*The shame I feel
must be apparent to all
who see my face*

*I cannot hide
the feelings of inadequacy
I cannot believe
that I have sinned again
I am so weak, so easily tempted*

*The remorse flows from me
as I fall on my knees
hiding my face on the floor*

*In agony I whisper,
"I am sorry, please, forgive me."*

Read Numbers 5: 5-7
" …'When a man or woman wrongs another in any way and so is unfaithful to the Lord, that person is guilty and must confess the sin he has committed.'"

Prayer:
Loving God, I confess that I have sinned. In my weakness, I disappointed You. I know how to act, Father, but I let myself slip. Forgive me, Lord, and take this sin away from me. I am so sorry for my weakness and for my sin. I know that with Your strength to support me, I can overcome any temptation I may encounter. I ask You to help me and I kneel before You with a humble, contrite heart as Your love covers my sin. Amen.

Conflict

*Turmoil
anguish
Pain
Bitterness*

*Confrontations building
and releasing
hiding
and storming in.*

*What waits
under the emotional upheaval
I cannot see.*

*Please,
open my eyes.*

Read 2 Timothy 2:24-26
" …**And the Lord's servant must not quarrel; instead, he must be kind to everyone, able to teach, not resentful."**

Prayer:
Lord, I am not sure which words to use to resolve the conflict that I am feeling. The pain and anger are real and ever present. Your word instructs me not to quarrel. Show me Your way through this problem and help me to resolve it as You would with grace and peace. If I cannot, then help me to wait until I can, and not add more bitterness in my weakness. Thank you, Lord. Amen.

Confusion

Where do I turn?
Whom do I trust?

How do I
discern the way
understand the truth?

Worry depletes
leaving me dry
and as weak as old bones in the bitter sun.

Take me now
calm my fears
lead me
on to Your perfect peace.

Read James 1:5-7
"…If any of you lacks wisdom, he should ask God, who gives generously to all without finding fault, and it will be given to him."

Prayer:
God of all, show me Your way. I am confused and unsure. I come to You asking, seeking wisdom and answers. Please guide me and help me discern Your will. I know You hear my plea and You will answer me. If I do not hear a definite yes or no, Lord, I will wait. For I know waiting on You is the best way for me to gain the wisdom that I need. Gratefully, I lift praise to You for all that You give to me. Amen.

Direction

*The road
before me
is an unknown
that I must travel down*

*Unaware.
Unafraid.
yet I hesitate
Which way do I choose?*

Indecision cripples me

*so I stop
and ask again
for guidance
and clear direction.*

Read Proverbs 3:5-6
"Trust in the Lord with all your heart and lean not on your own understanding; in all your ways acknowledge him and he will make your paths straight."

Prayer:
Lord, you have searched me and You know me better than I know myself. I do not know which way I am to go. I find myself at a cross roads and I have to make a decision. Lord, I come to You seeking Your will. You know what is best and perfect for me, and I do trust You with all my heart. Be with me, God, as I choose the direction You have for me to follow. I praise You and acknowledge You in all my ways. Amen.

Discernment

Decisions
weigh heavily
on my heart

the enormity of it all
overwhelms me

leaving me feeling helpless
Take me as your child

Oh God
lead me
to Your way.

Read Philippians 1: 9-11
"…So that you may be able to discern what is best and may be pure and blameless until the day of Christ."

Prayer:
Holy Spirit, dwell in me. Take away my confusion and show me the way You would have me to go, the life You would have me to lead. The enormity of the tasks before me, I find overwhelming. I ask You to break them down into small manageable parts for me to handle surrounded by Your loving grace, one decision at a time. Thank You, Loving Spirit, for Your help and counsel. Amen.

Discipline

Help me

when I need more
when I am unable to manage
when I go wrong

Correct me

Paths ahead loom
as unclear murky water
and lead me to errors

I do not want to do wrong intentionally
yet, in my haste
I can act rashly

Slow me down
correct my impulses.

Read Hebrews 12:5-12
"…Endure hardship as a discipline; God is treating you as sons…"

Prayer:
God, You are The Father of Creation, The Wise Counselor, and The Great I Am. You know what is best for me even when I think I am in control: I know I am not, but You are. Lord, guide me in Your path. Teach me Your ways that I may walk in Your direction. Let me know that this present path, that may seem unclear, is the purpose You have set out for me. Your discipline is for my good. As a father directs his children, direct me. Amen.

Doubt

Uncertainty cripples me
Did I understand correctly?

Am I sure?

Do I waiver back and forth?

Does the needle of doubt
prick at my heart
cause me to suspect,

to question,
to second guess,
what I know is truth?

Read James 1:6
"But when he asks, he must believe and not doubt, because he who doubts is like a wave of the sea, blown and tossed by the wind."

Prayer:
Lord God, help me to be strong in my faith. I know Your way is the perfect way, yet I am doubtful. I have tried to release my concerns to You and have faith and not waiver. I am finding it so difficult to trust and to believe that You hear me. I seek You, Lord, with all that I am. I ask You to take this doubt from me and show me what You have in store for me. I trust You. I give my doubt to You with gratitude that You will take care of me and love me through my pain and confusion. Amen.

Encouragement

*An outstretched hand
to clasp my hesitant one,*

*a hug given spontaneously,
a pat on the back
when I least expect it.*

*A slow smile from across a room,
A warm summer rain
filling my heart
with God's peaceful joy.*

Read Romans 15:5
"May the God who gives endurance and encouragement give you a spirit of unity among yourselves as you follow Christ Jesus…"

Prayer:
Dear Jesus, Your love and strength encourages me when I am weary and weak. Thank you, Lord. Help me to rely on that love and strength in any situation. Help me to know with out any doubts that You are my encourager. You want me to do well. Even more, Lord, help me to encourage others in the strength of Your love. Let me be the source of hope for those who are feeling hopeless. Fill my soul with Your encouragement and provide a chance for me to encourage someone today in Your name. Amen.

Faith

Assurance
The knowledge that I am watched over
by a loving God

The joy of heartfelt peace

The promise of tears wiped away
Hurts wrapped in love
Strength to move forward
one tiny step at a time

Faith as small as that
can do mighty things.

Read Matthew 17:18-21
"...I tell you the truth, if you have faith as small as a mustard seed, you can say to this mountain, 'Move from here to there' and it will move. Nothing will be impossible for you."

Prayer:
Dear Jesus, teach me to have the faith of which You speak. I can be so weak in my faith walk. Show me how to believe and to know that You are God of all, including the weak. By faith, You will strengthen me. Equip me for the work You have laid out for me to increase Your kingdom. I want to be strong, but I need Your help. Come to me now, Lord, and fill me with the power of Your Spirit so my faith can grow and I can pass that faith on to others. Amen.

Fear

Darkness and despair
walk behind me

threatening to overwhelm me
and render me helpless

I am so afraid

so tired
so weak
so vulnerable

Be still
Let God
soothe
calm
restore
as no other force can.

Read Psalm 91
"...You will not fear the terror of the night, nor the arrow that flies by day, nor the pestilence that stalks in the darkness, nor the plague that destroys at midday..."

Prayer:
Oh, God, I am so afraid. My fear consumes me and I do not know how to control it. I ask You to take this fear from me and to fill me with Your courage. I know that I can do all things with You as my rock and my encourager. Take me as I am, Lord, weak as a child. Build me up so that I can overcome my fears and move into the peace that You will give me. I ask You with a full and humble heart, encourage me, Father. Amen.

Forgiveness

I am sorry.
The words stick in my throat wanting to pour forth
Yet waiting somehow
I hold on to the pain and hurt

Why?

I forgive you.

I can whisper the words
I want to say them
but I am waiting for the "I am sorry"
that may never come

Then I remember
"Forgive others as I forgive you"

I am sorry. I forgive you.

The healing begins.

Read 2 Corinthians 5:17-21
"...Therefore, if anyone is in Christ, he is a new creation; the old has gone, the new has come!"

Prayer:
God, I have sinned against You alone. I am sorry with all my heart. I give the sin to You. Wipe it clean from my heart. I know I can't hold on to this sin, Lord, but if I try, please take it from me right now. I accept Your love and forgiveness, Lord, with a humble heart. Even more, I accept Your strength and power to forgive anyone I need to forgive, for in You I can do all things. Thank You for the freedom from sin. Thank You for loving me and for providing the strength to forgive in order to be Your ambassador and allow You to flow through me to others. Amen.

Gratitude

How wonderful are the things that you have done for me!
How can I ever praise you enough?

If I have my entire life, to eternity and back
I could not fill the depths of gratitude
for all that you have given to me!

for loving me when I was so much less than lovable
for providing for me in times of want and wealth

for my gifts and my faults for through them you teach me.

for Your grace,
peace, joy,
and abiding love.

Read Colossians 3:15-17
" ...And whatever you do, whether in word or deed, do it all in the name of the Lord Jesus, giving thanks to God the Father through him."

Prayer:
Father God, I thank You and I praise Your name for the many blessings You have given to me. I know that all things come from You and I am so awed by all that You have given to me. My voice rises in the morning to sing praises to You. I carry Your praise on my lips and in my heart all the day. I do not deserve the bounty of Your blessing, Lord, and I thank You with a full and overflowing heart for all that You give me. Your love is endless. Your unconditional love sustains me, and I will spread that love to everyone that I encounter this day. Amen.

Grief

The pain of loss

so real

I am immobilized

The everyday tasks seem impossible to perform

Will I ever be able to smile again?

Will the emptiness ever ease?

Will the hole that is my heart ever be full again?

How mighty is the hurt.

Read Isaiah 61:1-3
"... to comfort all who mourn and provide for those who grieve in Zion- to bestow on them a crown of beauty, instead of ashes, the oil of gladness instead of mourning, and a garment of praise instead of a spirit of despair."

Prayer:
Father God, You know the pain in my soul. I grieve with all that I am. The pain is ever present and ever real to me. I can hardly see the light of Your love. I am utterly down and troubled by the loss that I feel. Please, Father, comfort me. Hold me in Your loving, caring arms and provide a balm for my pain. I know that Your love will sustain me, even as I walk down this difficult path. You are there waiting to give me a spirit of praise. I do not need to have all the answers to why this happened, I need to rest in Your love and know that Your will is perfect. Even when I am in pain, Your love for me will carry me through. The pain is there, and so are You. Thank you, Lord, for weeping with me. Amen.

Guilt

*Shame and sorrow
stifle me like a heavy blanket
that I cannot shake off*

*weariness covers my soul
as the shame and the self doubt
take over*

*Why, I shout to myself, did I give in?
Why did I hurt once again?
-not only myself
but those I love,*

And You, Lord, my God,

Why?

Read Psalm 51:1-17
"Have mercy on me, O God, according to your unfailing love; according to your great compassion blot out my transgressions. Wash away all my iniquity and cleanse me from my sin…"

Prayer:
Oh, God, how sorry I am that I have sinned. I try to do what is right, but I am weak. I am so ashamed of my weakness. I want to hide myself from You and to pull away in my shame and sorrow. Your love for me seems so far away when I know that I disappoint You. Thank you for Your grace, which covers every sin that I commit. Please, I ask with a contrite heart, for Your grace to pour over me and wash away my guilt and my sin. Let Your love replace my weakness. Keep me, Father, from sinning again. Please forgive me and move me to accept Your forgiveness and grace. Strengthen me for the next trial and help me to be a better child of Yours. Amen.

Happiness

Joy fills my heart

flows up
from a well of living water

You alone, O God
can fill me with such holy joy

You alone, O God
can heal me
restore me

basking in Your presence
in the happiness of loving you.

Read Philippians 4:11-13
"I am not saying this because I am in need, for I have learned to be content whatever the circumstance…"

Prayer:
Dear God, teach me, as You did for Paul, to learn that true happiness comes from You. Help me not to look at things of this world or other people to find my happiness. I know that Your love is the key to true and lasting joy. I ask You to show me how to embrace that love even in the midst of a crisis. All things on this earth will pass away, but Your love and joy are eternal. Thank you, God for my happiness. Amen.

Harmony

A balance of life

all things coordinated

joined in perfection

that only comes from the perfect one, Jesus.

Guide me to that balance

as I seek to find peace

in harmony with you, my God,

at the pinnacle.

Read Romans 12:9-16
"…Live in harmony with one another."

Prayer:
Heavenly Father, I thank you for Your words of guidance on how to live my life. I strive to hear them completely, to take them into my heart, and to live at peace with my brothers and sisters. Please, help me today to remember Your words when I am faced with conflict, doubt, or fear. I can be assured that You want me to be in harmony. You will help me to achieve your peace that surpasses my understanding but is there to lift me up. Thank you, Father for loving me. Amen.

Healing

Despair

overwhelming and complete
takes over my heart, my soul, my mind.

I yield

not to the fears
But, to You, Lord
and Your perfect plan for me.

I submit myself to you
asking for complete healing

I praise you
I thank you, for loving me so much

I know you have this present pain under control

Read 1 Peter 2:23-25
"**...He himself bore our sins in his body on the tree, so that we might die to sin and live for righteousness; by his wounds you have been healed.**"

Prayer:
God, You are the great physician and the healer of all wounds to the flesh, to the spirit and to the soul. I am in need of healing, Lord. I come to You, weak with pain. I ask You to provide rest for me. I know Your will is perfect and my healing will come about as You see what is best for me. Giver of all, give to me what I need to sustain me as I wait. I thank you with all my being for sending Jesus to die so that I may live with You forever healed of all afflictions in the full glory of heaven. Amen.

Hope

*I can hold on
to a light
as small as a single lamp
to guide me*

because

my hope is in the Lord

who will send what I need

when I need it

at all times

I just have to ask

*The glow of Your light
is all I need.*

Read Psalm 42: 5-6
"Why are you so downcast, O my soul? Why so disturbed within me? Put your hope in God, for I will yet praise him, my Savior and my God…"

Prayer:
Holy Comforter, I am feeling so hopeless. I come to You with a heavy heart for I do not see a way out. I know that You have a plan for me that is perfect and I do not need to know every detail of that plan. I can rest on the assurance that You will be there for me, guide me, and lead me home to You at the end of the journey. Give me the hope of a future with You, Lord, and let me know that the present situation is but a step along that path. Amen.

Humility

You give to me all that I am
All that I have

I am nothing without You

Gifts

Talents

Strengths

are not my own but Yours, O God

I proclaim You as my Lord
and the giver of all

I thank You
from the depths of my being.

Read Micah 6:8
"He has showed you, O man, what is good. And what does the Lord require of you? To act justly and to love mercy and to walk humbly with your God."

Prayer:
Dear Father, show me how to do what You require of me with an attitude of humility, for all things that I have and all that I am comes from You. Help me to keep my pride in check and to give praise and honor to You for what I accomplish. I can often take the credit when I should give homage to You who has given so much to me. I thank you with a heart that is so blessed. I ask You to keep me humble and to know how very grateful I am for Your gifts and Your love. Amen.

Intervention

Enter in, O Holy Spirit

Hear my plea

Guide me

Heal me

Move in a small whisper

Rush in a mighty way

Take over for me

Where I cannot

Oh, Spirit, be my Comforter.

Read Romans 8:26-27
"…And he who searches our hearts knows the mind of the Spirit, because the Spirit intercedes for the saints in accordance with God's will."

Prayer:
Lord, I come to You with a heart that is filled with concern and with hope. I do not know how to solve this problem, but You do, Lord. I can rest assured that even when I am weak and feel helpless that You are strong and will carry the problem for me. I ask You to step in, Lord, and take over this burden for me. If I try to take it back, remind me that You are in charge, not me. I know that I cannot solve this alone, Lord, and that You will intervene and Your perfect solution will result. I praise Your name and thank You with a humble heart. Amen.

Jealousy

The feeling creeps in

at first
unacknowledged

just a slip of a thought

it grows

takes a life of its own

as envy overwhelms,

stifles and stops me

Take this from me!

I cannot bear

to feel this way.

Read Galatians 5:25-26
"Since we live by the Spirit, let us keep in step with the Spirit. Let us not become conceited, provoking and envying each other."

Prayer:
Holy Spirit, come to me. I feel so ashamed of my thoughts and feelings of wanting what another has. Why must I wait? Why must I do without when others seem to have so much? Speak to my jealous heart, Spirit, and cleanse these thoughts from me. I freely give them to You. I ask You to assure me that I am loved and that You have taken care of my needs. I know that I can rest assured that You are with me, guiding me to what is right for me. Your love for me is all that I need. Amen.

Joy

The radiance shines

from my soul

illuminating my face

lighting up the room

The love of God bubbles forth

overflowing

from the depths of who I am.

Joy is complete-
no matter the circumstance,

the sorrow or pain,

Unconditional happiness
wrapped in the love of God.

Read Psalm 126
"...The Lord has done great things for us and we are filled with joy."

Prayer:
God, You have filled the world with such beauty. I stand in awe of Your creation and majesty. I am filled to overflowing from the wealth of joy that You provide for me. Make me more aware of all that I pass on a daily basis. Show me the depth of joy even when sorrow looms. Allow Your joy that wells up inside me to overflow to everyone that I meet. There is no substitute for the joy of Your unconditional love and abounding grace. Your joy is my strength. Amen.

Knowledge

I am stopped

waiting for a sign

something tangible

I listen

I yield to You, O God

Fill my heart with Your wisdom

Show me Your way

that I may stay

in your will.

Help me to be fully armed

with all the knowledge I need

to move as You direct.

Read Proverbs 10:14
"Wise men store up knowledge, but the mouth of a fool invites ruin."

Prayer:
Lord, the knowledge that I need for living my life fully and completely is found in Your word and Your teachings. Guide me, Oh Lord, to the truths that are right for me. In every situation, give me the wisdom that I need. I seek the way You would have me to go, not my own stubborn course of action. Stop me, Lord, if I choose the wrong path. Lift me up and show me the source of knowledge that begins and ends with You. Amen

Longing

The peace of my spirit

is disturbed.

I long for a sign,

a message

to fulfill my soul.

I want what I cannot have

I search for what will give me peace,

knowing that You, God, are my hope

my solution.

Read Psalm 119: 81-87
"My soul faints with longing for your salvation, but I have put my hope in your word…"

Prayer:
Holy Spirit, I long for something to make my life easier, to give me comfort and provide a better way for me to live. I do not see this desire fulfilled and I am frustrated. I have prayed and prayed and see no answers. Please, Spirit, fill my need, end my longing, and ease my soul. I need help to put my hope in You, for in my weakest hours, I find myself resentful and full of self-pity. Take this longing from me and turn it to hope in You and in Your word. I long for You and Your perfect love more than I long for anything. Amen.

Loneliness

Alone

*I stand heavyhearted
burdened with a load to bear
that seems too heavy for one person*

Alone

the weight of my cares crush me

I fall

I wait

*for You have promised me
that You will carry me through
each day of my life*

I never have to be alone again.

Read Luke 5:16
"But Jesus often withdrew to lonely places and prayed."

Prayer:
Father God, the loneliness is overtaking me. I feel so lost and so alone. Even in prayer, I am having a hard time feeling Your presence. As I pray to You, I ask You to reach into my lonely places and fill them with Your grace and love. Help me to know that even when I am alone, You are there. Even when I am by myself, I am never alone. Fill me with Your presence and take this feeling of desolation away from me. I know You will never allow me to be alone. I come to You thankful, knowing Your love will fill my heart where it is empty. Please allow the lonely feeling to dull and replace it with Your perfect love. Amen.

Love

To give without expectation

To nurture

Guide

Steer

Admonish

Forgive

Over and over
To rely on the One and only God
Who loves every creature
Unconditionally
In perfect love.

Read 1 Corinthians 13
"...Love is patient, love is kind. It does not envy, it does not boast, it is not proud. It is not rude, it is not self-seeking, it is not easily angered, and it keeps no record of wrongs. Love does not delight in evil, but rejoices in the truth. It always protects, always trusts, always hopes, always perseveres..."

Prayer:
Loving Father, teach me how to love as You direct. Even more, teach me how to accept the love that You wish to pour out on me. I know that I am a sinner and that I can do nothing to earn Your love. I do not deserve it, yet You freely give love to me unconditionally and overflowing. Direct me, Father, how to love others in the same way so that I may fully love as You love me. Amen.

Overwhelmed

Lost and anxious
I struggle

Completion of only the minor duties
Overwhelms

I cannot lift myself
Above the pain

The confusion
Takes over

I am comforted to know

That You feel my pain too

And will provide a solution.

Deuteronomy 31:6
"Be strong and courageous. Do not be afraid or terrified because of them, for the Lord your God, goes with you; he will never leave you or forsake you."

Prayer:
God of all creation, You are with me through all of my life, the good and the bad. I am feeling like I cannot handle the stress that has been placed upon me. I am ready to give up. I cannot go on. Please, Father, come to me and help me. I ask You for a solution to this problem. Take the task before me and help me. Guide me to break it down into small manageable parts so that I can see how to solve this, as You would have me to solve it. I want to honor You. I thank you for Your help as my burden eases and I can move just one step closer to a solution. Amen.

Patience

Affirmation

Confirmation

Direction

Waiting

Totally giving up control over to God

who is all

knows all

reveals all

in His perfect time.

Read Ecclesiastes 7:8
"The end of a matter is better than its beginning, and patience is better than pride."

Prayer:
Father God, my patience is running out! I am feeling like I cannot go on. Please, give me a drink of the everlasting water to restore me and renew me so that I can be more patient in all situations. Let me come to Your well and draw from it when I feel my patience slipping. I can be assured that You will give me what I need if I only ask. I am asking now with a full heart for the renewing spirit of patience. Amen.

Perseverance

To go the distance

To keep on trying

even when the odds

against me seem larger than life

Taking the tasks ahead and

Bit by bit

Finishing one small part of the whole

Letting the Lord strengthen

Providing the tools needed

to complete me.

Read Hebrews 12:1-3
"Consider him who endured such opposition from sinful men, so that you will not grow weary and lose heart."

Prayer:
Wonderful Savior, You have given me the best gift, the grace and love of God for my sins. Sometimes I feel like giving up, Lord. I know that You felt this way too when You faced the cross. My cross pales in comparison to what You suffered so that I could have eternal life. Help me to change my attitude of despair into one of hope. I keep trying to become the person You want me to be and to complete the tasks You set before me. I know I can do this with You to walk beside me guiding me along the way. Amen.

Praise

The glory of God

Proclaimed

In the iridescent leaf,

Delicate feather,

Breathtaking flower,

Every unique face

How majestic!

How awe-filled I stand

One small person

a part of life, earth, sky and seas

Praises rise to the heavens
Alleluia, Amen!

Read Exodus 15:1-2
"...He is my God and I will praise him, my father's God, and I will exalt him."

Prayer:
Heavenly Father, You are the Most High. Your glory and splendor are beyond my imagination. I magnify You and praise Your holy name. I lift my voice in the morning and sing Your praises all the day. As I rest at night, I give thanks to You for all that You have provided for me. You are my King. I worship Your majesty and I glorify Your name. Your praise is in my heart and ever on my lips. With humble gratitude I exalt You. Amen.

Renewal

Cycles of life

Over and over

Provide the faith

to remain steady and strong

Restore my soul

Regain my focus

Renew my hope

in my Lord

and my Savior.

Read Isaiah 57:10
"You were wearied by all your ways, but you would not say, 'It is hopeless.' You found renewal of your strength and so you did not faint."

Prayer:
O, God, there are so many times when I cannot find the strength I need to go on. I feel so very helpless and weak in the face of my problems. Take this from me, God, and help me to lean on Your arm as I walk through this valley. All I have to do is take the next step. I know You are holding me up even when I cannot hold up myself. Thank You for loving me so that I can renew my strength and walk with You once again. Amen.

Resentment

Why?

climbs into my thoughts
takes over my reasoning

I do not deserve
to be treated this way

Why?

The anger settles in the pit of my soul
simmering
threatening to boil over into rage

I cry out
with all that I am.

Ease the pain,
Please, help me, Lord.

Read 2 Timothy 2:22-26
"...And the Lord's servant must not quarrel; instead, he must be kind to everyone, able to teach, not resentful..."

Prayer:
Dear Holy Spirit, come to me and ease these feelings of bitterness and offense. I know that I have a right to be resentful over these circumstances, but if I hold onto the resentment, it consumes me and I hurt even more. Take Your blanket of comfort and wrap me in Your arms. Let the feeling that I want to hold on to dissipate and flow from me. You are my Comforter and my Restorer. Thank you. Amen.

Rest

Softly falling rain

A gentle wind

Cheerful calls of children

Bright sunshine to warm winter faces

A small drink of God's goodness

Restores

Renews

Refills

Provides the rest we need.

Read Matthew 11:28-30
"Come to me, all you who are weary and burdened, and I will give you rest. Take my yoke upon you and learn from me, for I am gentle and humble in heart and you will find rest for your souls. For my yoke is easy and my burden is light."

Prayer:
Dear Jesus, I am worn out. My body feels drained and I cannot move another step. I come to You with a weary soul in need of restoration and peace. Come to me, dear Lord, and renew my mind, my heart, my body and my soul. I take Your comfort as a strong shoulder to lean on and wrap myself up in its peace. I know You are the provider of all. You carry my burdens with You. As I release them, the rest that I need comes too. Thank you, Loving Lord, thank you. Amen.

Salvation

Your love for me

Is beyond comprehension

Forgive my limited capacity

to understand the depth of love

that would lay down

the life of a Son

so that I can be forgiven.

Loved to the core of my soul

no matter how weak and sinful I am

The power of the cross
saves and forgives
A gift freely given

I fall to my knees praising my God.

Read 1 Thessalonians 5:9
"For God did not appoint us to suffer wrath, but to receive salvation through our Lord Jesus Christ."

Prayer:
Precious Jesus, You suffered and died for my sins. I cannot comprehend that kind of sacrifice and love. It is more than I can understand. I ask You to come into my heart, and I accept you as my Lord and my Savior. Let Your love heal my wounds. Show me how to accept Your love unconditionally so I may pass that same love on to others. I rest assured that You hold a place in heaven for me. I thank You for Your gift of love that is everlasting. Amen.

Strength

Weakness saps my reserve
to the empty point
I cannot go on.

I am weary to my bones

small tasks seem to take so much effort.

I sit and wait

letting the love of God creep in and
fill the hollow spaces with renewed vision
bit by bit

He lifts me up

I can do all things

by His mighty strength!

Read Isaiah 40: 29-31
"...but those who hope in the Lord will renew their strength. They will soar on wings like eagles; they will run and not grow weary, they will walk and not be faint."

Prayer:
Heavenly Father, I am weak. I need to wait on You, Lord, as Your word directs. Please give me the strength to allow You to lead me through this. I am not strong enough to handle this problem alone, Lord, and I rely on You to guide me and prepare me for the task that lies ahead. Renew my strength, Father, that in my weariness, I may not stumble. I thank you. Amen.

Temptation

A small voice, a whispered suggestion
A random thought enters
Unaware

And repeats

Urges

Cajoles

Shouts

In my weakness
I do not want to give in

Help me

Strengthen me
My Lord and My Savior.

Read Matthew 26:41
"Watch and pray so that you will not fall into temptation. The spirit is willing, but the body is weak."

Prayer:
Dear Lord, help me to resist the temptation before me. I am willing to try, Lord, but I am so weak in the face of this obstacle. I ask that You give me the insight to avoid the situations that may cause me to be tempted. In my weakness, I do not want to sin. If I cannot avoid the situation, help me, Lord, to be strong in You, to lean on You, so that You may lead me out of the danger I face. I know that You have empathy for me as only You, my Lord, can feel the temptations I feel and resist. Teach me to resist, give me the power to stop when I am tempted. I fall on my knees calling on your name. Amen.

Thanksgiving

Humble adoration for all that You are

all that You provide for me

I am nothing without my gifts

Everything that You, my heavenly Father, offer me

From morning to rest time,

You give me all that I need if I but ask

With a heart that overflows

I thank you, Lord, for making me

as I am

for loving me in my imperfection

for providing all that I need to praise and honor You.

Read Psalm 100
"…Enter his gates with thanksgiving and his courts with praise; give thanks to him and praise his name…"

Prayer:
All glory and majesty are given to You, God, the most high. I sing Your praises with a joyful heart. I praise you for the many blessings you provide. You are so awesome and so wonderful! My heart is filled with the glory of You! I kneel before You with reverence and ask Your grace to flow over me and fill me with Your abiding love that endures forever. Amen.

Worry

Nagging doubt

Eats away at my soul

Corrodes my faith

tears away hope

Why can't I remember how precious I am in Your eyes?

That You have everything

in Your control?

I release the worry

Let go and

Let You

take care of me.

Read Matthew 6:25-27
"...Who by worrying can add a single hour to his life?..."

Prayer:
Holy Spirit, come to me now and take this worry away from me. I try to give my doubts to You but I take them back again. I know that You have my fears and my anxiety under Your control and that I need not fear the unknown. You are the Wise Counselor and You know my way even before I ask. Let Your peace and calm assurance flow over me and let the worry I feel ease and disappear. I surrender all concerns to You, most gracious God. Amen.

Worship

Arms uplifting
Voices uniting
Instruments resounding

Praise to the Lord

Praise to the King

Praise to the Most High Deliverer

Praise To You

The Prince of Peace

The Holy One

In humble adoration
Your children praise You
Our Holy Father.

Read Psalm 95:
"...Come, let us bow down in worship, let us kneel before the Lord our Maker; for he is our God and we are the people of his pasture, the flock under his care..."

Prayer:
God of all, You are the most high, the Holy One, whom I adore. I come to You filled this day with reverence for all Your creation. You have formed the beings, all the creatures, the beauty and splendor of the land before us. How great is Your majesty! I worship You, God, with all that I am. I am humbled and awe struck by the creation, power and glory You have formed. Even more than that, I am so thankful for the grace, forgiveness and love that You pour out on me. I love you, God, with all that I am. Amen.

Appendix

You may want to explore these questions as a way to increase your faith. The answers will be unique to you and will help you better understand yourself and our amazing God. There is not one wrong or right answer. You will receive the answer you need according to God's perfect plan. Explore on your own but you may feel led to conduct or participate in the small group study. I have written a leader's guide for this to help you increase your faith through studying with others.

Searching questions for your own study or use with the small group study session:

Session one and two:
You will explore the topics of acceptance, change, direction, discernment and harmony.
- Did you find an answer to a question of direction?
- What specifically did you learn from God's word as an answer to prayer for direction?
- What is the difference between acceptance and change?
- How do you tell if an answer is God's or yours?
- What is the benefit of achieving harmony in your life?

Session three:
You will explore the topics of adoration, encouragement, gratitude, happiness and praise.
- When have you felt the most humbled by the majesty of God?
- How do you feel the encouragement you need to live your life as a bold Christian?
- How do you express gratitude even in the midst of pain?
- How is it possible to have happiness at all times?
- When do you feel like praising God the most?

Session four:
You will explore the topics of anger, fear, grief, jealousy, and resentment.
- When has anger caused you to act irrationally?
- When have you been more afraid of the thought of something than the actual event?
- Why is grief so difficult?
- What are positives about the process of grief?
- When can jealousy and resentment teach you a better way?

Session five:
You will explore the topics of blessing, faith, hope, love and thanksgiving.
- What do you consider to be a blessing from God?
- How do you know it is from Him?
- What is the best way to grow your faith?
- How do you keep your hope when tragedy strikes?
- How can you embrace the mighty love that God has for you?
- Why is it difficult to accept God's love?
- What keeps you from loving others as God loves you?
- What is the difference between thanksgiving and giving?

Session six: You will explore the topics of comfort, knowledge, patience, perseverance and strength.
- How have you felt the comfort of God through others?
- How can you gain knowledge?
- When do you need to pray for patience?
- How can you keep on trying when times are difficult?
- How can you feel strong when you are so very weak?

Session seven:
You will explore the topics of conflict, confusion, doubt, guilt and feeling overwhelmed.
- How are you to handle conflict within the church or other Christians?
- What are you to do when you are confused?
- How can you overcome doubt?
- What causes you to feel guilty?
- How does God direct you to deal with guilt?
- What is the best way to proceed when you are overwhelmed?

Session eight:
You will explore the topics of discipline, intervention, longing, renewal and rest.
- When is it hard to accept God's discipline?
- How do you intervene on the part of a family member or some one who does not know the Lord?
- How can you satisfy your longings to be only for what God wants and allows?
- Why are rest and renewal so important?
- How can you make them a priority?

Session nine:
You will explore the topics of forgiveness, healing, loneliness, temptation and worry.
- Why is it so difficult to forgive those who are not sorry for their behavior?
- How can you prevent your healing if you hold on to unforgiving thoughts?
- What are some cures for loneliness?
- How can you resist temptation?
- How does worry affect you?
- How can you keep from worrying?

Session ten:
You will explore the topics of confession, humility, joy, salvation and worship.
- What does a confession allow to happen for you?
- What are you hiding that needs to be put before God?
- How can you remain humble when you are seeking praise, recognition and gratitude?
- What is the difference between happiness and joy?
- Have you prayed the prayer of salvation?
- What is keeping you from praying it?
- What changes will you make to worship God with all your being?

Notes:

Notes:

www.ingramcontent.com/pod-product-compliance
Lightning Source LLC
Chambersburg PA
CBHW020021050426

42450CB00005B/590